The Complete Slow Cooker Recipe Cookbook #2021

Quick and Delicious Recipes for Everyone incl. Vegan and Vegetarian Recipes

Sarah K. Parker

Table of Contents

Introduction

It's without doubt that there is a myriad of cooking appliances in the world right now. The variety of cooking techniques and recipes have made it necessary for companies to come up with appliances that execute those rare techniques with perfection. It becomes a daunting task to decide on the right appliance for your kitchen, given the vast variety you are supposed to select from. Right from pressure cookers, air fryers, instant pots among others, it gets even more confusing to pick the right one for your kitchen. Amid all this variety, one appliance that should not miss in any modern kitchen is the slow cooker. This sleek appliance is here to ensure that you cook your food hands-free and also enjoy all the rich flavor that comes from the great spices. This text will bring to the fore all you need to know about slow cookers including the do's and don'ts, best practices when using a slow cooker among others. Tag along!

What Is a Slow Cooker?

A slow cooker is essentially a countertop appliance that cooks food under lower temperatures as compared to other cooking techniques. In this sense, a slow cooker makes it possible to have unattended cooking for longer periods. What is particularly interesting about this appliance is the fact that most quickly prepared meals can easily be cooked in this sleek appliance, but you get to enjoy the benefits that come with preparing meals slowly under lower temperatures.

How the Slow Cooker Works

To understand how the slow cooker works, it is essential to break down the design of a regular slow cooker. It consists of a circular glazed ceramic cooking pot surrounded by a metallic housing that contains an electrical cooking element. A majority of these appliances feature glass lids that fit snug on the ridge atop the pot. It is quite impressive that the contents inside the pot remain at atmospheric pressure despite the vapor that generates inside. This is made possible because of the groove where condensed vapor collects creating a zone of low pressure sealing in the lid even better. This brilliant technique makes meal preparation safe because you don't run the risk of sudden pressure release which is possible with the pressure cooker. Many slow cookers are equipped with more than one cooking setting, for instance, the low, high, or keep warm among others for modern versions. The low setting will allow your food to cook for a significantly longer period as compared to the high setting. The keep-warm feature will allow your food to stay warm after cooking until when you are ready to serve. Modern models come with other multifunctional settings including functions like browning and even others serve as pressure cookers. Not having to use extra pans or appliances to perform these tasks will not only save you time but also the unnecessary dishes to wash thereafter.

Getting the Right Slow Cooker for You

Slow cookers come in different sizes and sophistication, how do you decide on the right one for you? This is the million-dollar question that is often a pain in the neck! However, fret not, here are a few tips that will point you in the right direction if you are having a hard time deciding which type is best for you.

Size

One fundamental aspect that you have to consider is the size of the pot relative to the average size of your regular meals. You will get slow cooking appliances as small as 1.5-quart to others as big as 8-quarts. The decision on what size is best for you will entirely lie on the size of your meals which is often determined by the size of your household.

Footprint

Well, it is no news that the countertop and cabinet space is a rare commodity that is hard to come by and also never enough. Before getting yourself a slow cooker there are several questions you will need to ask yourself beforehand. How much space can I spare on my countertop? Is the cooker too tall for the cabinet? Will it take up all the space in the cabinet? These are just but a few of the necessary questions that you ought to ask yourself before deciding on the one to take home.

Features

It's time to consider the sophistication of the particular slow cooker. Here, you will have to decide on whether you want to perform only the slow cooking function on your appliance. Remember some older models only offer slow cooking functions exclusively. However, if you want more activity and functions out of your cooker, for instance, browning, air frying, and also searing, we prefer you to go for modern models that will make this a reality. We prefer models that have computerized temperature control and monitoring functions. Be sure to get one with the keep warm feature which is absolutely necessary.

Programmable functions

Programmable features serve to make your work a notch easier. One feature that comes in handy for all you busy folks is the delayed cooking function. This feature will allow you to start cooking without pressing any button. With this function, you will be able to time your meal prep without having to be there physically. However, this function should be used within two hours if you are cooking meat. Bacteria act on meat faster when left under room temperature therefore increasing your chances of falling ill.

Preparing Different Meals
for Slow Cooking

Beans

Canned beans are rather easy and straightforward when it comes to. However, ensure that you put them in the last 30 minutes of your cooking to maintain their shape while warming up. Dried beans on the other hand need some preparation before cooking. It is recommended to soak them overnight. Don't add in any sugar, salt, or any additive at the beginning because it makes them difficult to tender up.

Vegetables

When it comes to vegetables, root veggies, for instance, potatoes cook longer than meat. So it is wise to cut them into smaller chunks and put them at the base of the cooker closest to the heat source. Introduce the leafy veggies in the slow cooker in the last 30 minutes of your cooking because they cook fast.

Meat

Chop the roasts into smaller chunks for easy tendering and even cooking. Remove the fatty bits of meat before cooking because it often causes overcooking due to heat retention. Always brown meat beforehand to give it some color.

Fish and SeaFood

Introduce seafood and fish towards the last hour of cooking. They tender up so fast and you don't want them to break down into the broth.

Handy Slow Cooker Tips

Prep the Night Before

For all you busy folks, it is good practice to prepare for slow cooking the night before especially if your mornings are busy. Put everything in the slow cooker at night and store it in the refrigerator overnight. In the morning all you have to do is to get the dish out of the fridge and let it stay for 20 minutes before switching it on since it should be as close to room temperature as possible.

Go for Cheap Cuts

One thing that you will learn down the line is that cheap cuts cook perfectly on the slow cooker. Get that pork shoulder, chicken thighs, lamb shoulders, or beef brisket going on in your slow cooker. Another tip is that you could cut down on the amount of meat since slow cooking permeates the meaty flavor throughout the entire meal. So go heavy on the veggies instead.

Cut Off Fat Before Slow Cooking Meat

Oil is not necessary for a slow cooker; your food won't burn provided you have enough moisture to work with. Different from deep frying, fat won't drain away during the cooking process so cut off the fatty parts lest you get pools of fat on your broth. Remember getting rid of the fat will mean that you get a healthier outcome which will be just as tasty.

Go Easy on the Liquids When Using a Slow Cooker

The slow cooker is designed with a tight-fitting lid which means water loss through evaporation is eliminated. With this in mind, only use half of the water you would use on a regular recipe. The water should just cover the veggies and meat. Never overfill the slow cooker since the meal won't cook quite as good, and also fluids might start leaking from the top. Ideally, the water in the pot should be ½ or ¾ full, not more than that!

Thicken Your Sauces with Flour

Fluids in the slow cooker hardly reduce and at the same time again, it hardly thickens. So, to achieve a thick sauce, you need a few tricks up your sleeve. You could coat your meat with flour preferably seasoned before putting it into the slow cooker. Alternatively, you could mix one or two teaspoons of cornflour with some cold water to a thick paste. Stir through the contents in the slow cooker before continuing with the cooking.

Make a Habit of Using the Low Setting

Many dishes prepared in the slow cooker benefit heavily from the low heat in bringing out the rich taste of the ingredients used. Moreover, you will be able to prepare your meals even when you have to step out for some errands for the day. However, most modern versions have the stay warm feature that will keep your food warm after cooking. Don't miss out on the rich and tasty flavors that come along with cooking using the low setting.

Cut Down Your Preparation Time

The idea behind slow cooking is easy cooking, therefore, whenever you are scouting for new recipes for your Saturday dinner, avoid those with many pre- requirements. In fact, most stews have zero to little preparation requirements. However, frying your onions before cooking in the slow cooker, the flavor is nicer than when put in raw. Also, it would be nice to brown the meat beforehand to get that nice appealing color that would otherwise be impossible to achieve in a slow cooker.

Cleaning the Slow Cooker

Similar to any other appliance in your kitchen, cleaning the slow cooker will ensure you get the best out of your appliance every time you put it to use. Furthermore, cleaning is the only care practice that you can actually count on if increasing the life of your appliance is anything to go by. Every kitchen appliance is made different which means that cleaning should also be done differently. So how do you clean your slow cooker?

- Well, it goes without saying that you have to unplug your appliance from the sauce of electricity before you start cleaning. Water and electricity are not a good mix, unplug, to avoid any electrical hazard.

- Some removable parts of the slow cooker could be dishwasher friendly, for instance, the glass lids and the removable stoneware. So, check with your manufacturer before going ahead and use the dishwasher every part.

- If your slow cooker does not have dishwasher-friendly parts, here are some of the guidelines when handwashing your appliance:

- Never submerge or immerse the heating element in water or any fluid for that matter.

- Always ensure the stoneware is cool before washing in cold water.

- Stay clear of any abrasive cleaning agent to remove spots or stains rather use vinegar or any non-abrasive alternative.

- Make use of soft cloths and sponges to clean and remove stubborn stains from your appliance.

Similar to that cluttered garage that you promise yourself every day to sort out, your slow cooker too, needs a deep clean regularly. What other time than on those lazy weekends that you don't need to use your slow cooker! Get yourself in the cleaning mood, take out those gloves, and follow the steps below for a deep clean:

- First, fill the cooker with water above the leftover line.

- Pour in a handful of distilled white vinegar, increase the amount of vinegar according to the size of the slow cooker.

- Pour in 1 cup of baking soda gradually as the bubbles die down.

- Now, set the slow cooker on low, cover, and let it heat up for 1 hour.

- After one hour, remove the lid, allow the appliance to cool before washing with a sponge and warm water with some soap.

- Allow it to dry on the counter.

Breakfast Recipes

The Slow Cooker Veggie Omelet

Time: 2 hours 10 minutes | Servings 8
Kcal 166, Carbs 5g/0.17oz, Fats 11g/0.39oz, Proteins 12g/0.42oz, Fiber 1g/0.035oz

INGREDIENTS

- 2 cloves of minced garlic
- 8 large whole eggs
- 1 finely chopped yellow small onion
- 125ml/½ a cup of milk
- 1 diced small red pepper
- 32g/¼ cup of grated parmesan cheese
- 128g/1 cup of broccoli florets

- A pinch of salt
- 2g/½ a teaspoon of chili powder
- Freshly ground pepper
- 2g/½ a teaspoon of garlic powder
- 2g/½ a teaspoon of dried Italian seasoning

Garnish

- Freshly chopped parsley
- 128g/1 cup of shredded cheddar cheese
- Finely diced onions

DIRECTIONS

1. Begin by applying a light coat of cooking spray to the slow cooker before keeping it aside.

2. Using a good-sized mixing bowl, put in the milk, eggs, parmesan cheese, garlic powder, chili powder, salt, Italian seasoning, and pepper then whisk everything together.

3. To the inserts of the slow cooker, put in the broccoli florets, minced garlic, chopped onions, and diced pepper. Pour in the egg mixture and toss to combine.

4. Now cook in the slow cooker for 2 hours. Remember to start checking for readiness 1 hour 30 minutes into the cooking.

5. You will know whether your omelet is done if it is all nice and set.

6. When almost set, top with cheddar cheese and cook some more till all the cheese has melted.

7. Switch off the cooker once done and allow the omelet to cool for a few minutes before garnishing with the chopped parsley and diced onions.

8. Divide into 8 pieces then serve!

Slow Cooker Oatmeal with Crispy Bacon

Time: 3 hours 5 minutes | Servings 4
Kcal 250, Carbs 25g/0.88oz, Fats 13g/0.46oz, Proteins 9.5g/0.33oz, Fiber 6g/0.21oz

INGREDIENTS

- Oatmeal
- 40g/1.5oz of uncured nitrate-free bacon strips
- 250ml/1 cup of water
- 160g/1¼ cups of gluten-free rolled oats
- 500ml/2 cups of plain almond milk
- 15ml/1 tablespoon of olive oil
- 180ml/¾ cup of broth

- 128g/1 cup of diced and peeled squash
- 4g/1 teaspoon of red pepper flakes
- 34g/2 tablespoons of flaxseeds
- 32g/¼ cup of parmesan
- 4g/1 teaspoon of sea salt
- 64g/½ a cup of sliced cherry tomatoes
- A pinch of black pepper
- 32g/¼ cup of sliced red onions

Toppings

- Optional pouched or fried egg
- 1 sliced avocado
- A pinch of pepper
- Steamed spinach
- Cooked onion and crispy bacon

- Red pepper flakes
- Parmesan cheese shavings
- Microgreens

1. In a slow cooker, combine the tomato slices, oil, flax seeds, diced squashes, oats, garlic, milk, seasoning, broth, and the parmesan.

2. Combine everything well and set your slow cooker on high to cook for 3 hours or low to cook for 5 hours depending on your preference.

3. Remember to stir and scrape the sides of the cooker every hour only if you use real cheese.

4. If you want to achieve a lighter consistency, add ¼ cup of water or broth in the last stages of your cooking.

5. When almost done, bring the oven to a temperature of 176°C/350°F then line the baking tray with parchment paper or foil.

6. Arrange the bacon strips and sliced onions on the tray then allow cooking for 15 minutes till nice and crispy.

7. Mix the extra bacon grease in the oats then serve into bowls and choose a topping of your choice from the list above.

Slow Cooker Creamy Banana French Toast

Time: 3 hours 30 minutes | Servings 6
Kcal 313, Carbs 24g/0.85oz, Fats 22g/0.78oz, Proteins 8g/0.28oz, Fiber 2g/0.07oz

INGREDIENTS

- Maple syrup
- 1 (25cm/10-inch) stale French baguette sliced into 2cm/1-inch slices
- 64g/½ a cup of pecans
- 2 bananas and some more for serving
- 17g/2 tablespoons of thinly sliced butter
- 3 lightly beaten eggs
- A pinch of nutmeg
- 375ml/1½ cups of milk
- 4g/1 teaspoon of ground cinnamon
- 32g/¼ cup of light brown sugar
- 2ml/½ a teaspoon of pure vanilla extract

DIRECTIONS

1. Using either butter or cooking spray, coat the insides of your cooker lightly.
2. Spread both sides of the bread with a generous amount of cream cheese before carefully arranging them in a single layer at the bottom of the slow cooker.
3. Mash 2 bananas in a good-sized mixing bowl before adding in the beaten eggs, vanilla, sugar, milk, cinnamon, and nutmeg.
4. Mix everything up until well combined.
5. Empty the milk mixture over the bread slices before pressing the bread into the liquid. Allow everything to sit and settle for 30 minutes or up to 5 hours. Note that the liquid shouldn't submerge the bread slices rather cover ¾ of the bread level.
6. Place the butter slices on top of the bread slices.
7. Cook in your slow cooker for 3 hours on the low setting or 2 to 2½ hours on the high setting.
8. Once cooked, top with the chopped pecans, maple syrup, and banana slices to garnish and serve while warm.

Chocolate Cherry Steel Cut Oatmeal

Time: 8 hours 10 minutes | Servings 10
Kcal 387, Carbs 67g/2.36oz, Fats 8g/0.28oz, Proteins 13g/0.46oz, Fiber 8g/0.28oz

INGREDIENTS

- ◆ Oatmeal
- ◆ A pinch of kosher salt
- ◆ 500ml/2 cups of 2% milk
- ◆ 2g/½ a teaspoon of almond extract
- ◆ 500ml/2 cups of water
- ◆ 60ml/¼ cup of maple syrup
- ◆ 128g/1 cup of steel-cut oats
- ◆ 28g/1oz of chopped unsweetened baker's chocolate
- ◆ 42g/⅓ a cup of dried tart cherries
- ◆ 34g/2 tablespoons of unsweetened cocoa powder
- ◆ Cherry sauce
- ◆ 1g/¼ a teaspoon of almond extract
- ◆ 190g/1½ cups of frozen tart cherries

- ◆ 30ml/2 tablespoons of water

DIRECTIONS

1. In a 4-quart slow cooker, combine the ingredients of the oatmeal and mix thoroughly.
2. Now put the mixture in the slow cooker and cover.
3. Set the cooker on low heat and allow cooking for 8 hours preferably overnight. If you are using a modern version of the cooker, keep the stay warm feature on so that your breakfast stays warm after cooking is done.
4. When you wake up, mix all the cherry sauce in a small saucepot. Stir over medium heat.
5. Allow the mixture to simmer before cooking for an additional 7 minutes till the sauce is nice and thick.
6. Now, check on your oatmeal and add in some milk if it is thicker than you prefer and stir.
7. Serve the oatmeal into bowls before topping with the warm cherry sauce and enjoy!

Slow Cooker Cinnamon Rolls

Time: 2 hours 30 minutes | Servings 10 cinnamon rolls
Kcal 140, Carbs 21g/0.74oz, Fats 5.4g/0.19oz, Proteins 1.8g/0.06oz, Fiber 0.6g/0.02oz

INGREDIENTS

- 345g/2¾ cups of all-purpose flour
- 180ml/¾ cup of whole milk
- 1 egg
- 10g/2½ teaspoons of instant yeast
- 60g/4 tablespoons of unsalted, melted, and slightly cooled butter
- 55g/ ¼ cup and 1 teaspoon of divided granulated sugar

For the filling

- 67g/⅓ a cup of granulated sugar
- 72g/5 tablespoons of very soft unsalted butter
- 17g/1 tablespoon of ground cinnamon

For the icing

- 30ml/2 tablespoons of milk
- 150g/1¼ cups of confectioner's sugar
- 30ml/2 tablespoons of pure maple syrup

DIRECTIONS

1. Begin by making the dough. Bring the milk to warm up over medium heat.
2. Pour the milk into a large mixing bowl before adding in the yeast and 17ml/1 tablespoon of granulated sugar and mix.
3. Cover the mixture and allow it to settle for 5-10 minutes till the yeast gets foamy.
4. Once this is done, add in the salt, eggs, butter, 32g/¼ cup of sugar, butter, and 2 cups of flour. Using a hand mixer, stir and combine everything up.
5. If the dough is still wet, add in the remaining ¼ cup of flour gradually as you whisk till it gets nice and firm.
6. Now, knead the dough on a floured surface for one minute before letting it rest for 10 minutes.
7. Meanwhile, line the bottom of the cooker with parchment paper (greased).
8. Once the dough settles for 10 minutes, roll it out into a rectangle before spreading the soft butter atop.
9. Now combine the cinnamon and sugar before sprinkling on top. Roll the dough neatly and tightly before slicing into 10 pieces.
10. Arrange the rolls atop the parchment paper, put a paper towel beneath the lid of the cooker to keep the condensed water away from the cooking rolls.
11. Set your slow cooker on high and allow the rolls to cook till done which should be about 2 hours.

12. Once cooked, remove from the cooker by simply lifting the parchment paper.
13. To make the glaze, combine the confectioners' sugar, milk, and maple syrup then mix till even.
14. Pour over the warm cinnamon rolls before serving.

Slow Cooker Egg Scramble

Time: 5 hours 5 minutes | Servings 6
Kcal 846, Carbs 48g/1.69oz, Fats 57g/2.01oz, Proteins 34g/1.2oz, Fiber 4g/0.14oz

INGREDIENTS

- 51g/3 tablespoons of diced chives
- 12 large eggs
- Cooking spray
- 800g/28oz bag of frozen potatoes
- Pepper and salt
- 450g/16oz of shredded Cheddar-Monterey Jack cheese blend
- 64g/½ a cup of heavy whipping cream

DIRECTIONS

1. Generously coat the insides of the slow cooker with the cooking spray beforehand.

2. Now, put in the frozen potatoes and top with ¼ of the grated Cheddar-Monterey Jack cheese blend.

3. In a large mixing bowl, crack the eggs and whisk till they are nice and get a uniform color. Pour in the heavy whipping cream and stir in together with the eggs before pouring the mixture into the slow cooker.

4. Put in the remainder of the cheese. Be sure to keep the cheese off the walls of the cooker to prevent premature and excessive browning.

5. Set your cooker to low then allow cooking for 5 to 8 hours depending on the brand of the slow cooker you have. If it is your first time using the cooker, you should always be flexible as far as the cooking time is concerned.

6. You will know your egg scramble is ready once the top begins to brown.

7. Remove from the cooker and garnish with the fresh chives before serving.

Slow Cooker Peach Cobbler Oatmeal

Time: 8 hours | Servings 6-8
Kcal 324, Carbs 38g/1.34oz, Fats 18g/0.63oz, Proteins 4g/0.140z, Fiber 3g/0.1oz

INGREDIENTS

- 1 can of coconut cream
- 190g/1½ cups of steel-cut oats
- 32g/½ a cup of coconut sugar
- 2½L/6 cups of unsweetened coconut milk
- 2g/½ a teaspoon of cinnamon
- 6 large and chopped peaches
- 64g/½ a cup of unsweetened coconut flakes

DIRECTIONS

1. Begin by greasing the insides of the slow cooker with a light coat of coconut oil.

2. Put in the oats, coconut sugar, coconut milk, cinnamon, coconut flakes, and peaches into a mixing bowl and combine evenly. Now empty the mixture into the slow cooker.

3. Depending on your preference and the type of slow cooker you have, set it on low and cook for 8 hours or put the cooker on high and cook for 4 hours.

4. Stir all the ingredients for 5 minutes or more until they combine evenly and thickens.

5. Once done, serve by scooping the desired amounts into a serving bowl and top with some coconut cream.

6. You can store your oatmeal for a week in the fridge.

7. If stored, reheat before serving by adding some coconut milk and heating your meal in a microwave.

Cheesy Ham Slow Cooker Breakfast Casserole

Time: 4 hours 20 minutes | Serves 12
Kcal 548, Carbs 15g/0.53oz, Proteins 35g/1.23oz, Fats 37g/1.3oz, Fiber 1g/0.03oz

INGREDIENTS

- 500g/4 cups of shredded cheddar cheese
- 12 whole eggs
- 1 chopped onion
- 250ml/1 cup of 2% milk
- 250g/2 cups of fully cooked ham cubes
- 4g/1 teaspoon of salt
- 850g/30oz package of frozen shredded hash browns
- 2g/½ a teaspoon of pepper

DIRECTIONS

1. Using a good-sized mixing bowl, combine pepper, milk, eggs, and salt then mix thoroughly till even.
2. Grease the insides of the slow cooker using a generous amount of oil.
3. Now, arrange ⅓ of the hash browns at the bottom of the slow cooker followed by ham, onions, and cheese in that order.
4. Arrange the layers twice in a similar fashion.
5. Drizzle the egg mixture atop the stack before putting it in the refrigerator over the night or you could also cook immediately.
6. Close the slow cooker and allow cooking using the Low setting for 4 to 5 hours or until the casserole edges start to brown.
7. When cooked, turn off the cooker before removing your casserole.
8. Allow cooling for roughly 30 minutes before serving.

Slow Cooker Breakfast Potatoes

Time: 4 hours 15 minutes | Servings 8
Kcal 192, Carbs 32g/1.13oz, Fats 6g/0.21oz, Proteins 4g/0.14oz, Fiber 3g/0.1oz

INGREDIENTS

- Black pepper and Kosher salt
- 1.3kg/3 lbs. of quartered red baby potatoes
- 30ml/2 tablespoons of extra virgin olive oil
- 1 diced and seeded green bell pepper
- 34g/2 tablespoons of diced unsalted butter
- 1 diced and seeded red bell pepper
- 8g/2 teaspoons of smoked paprika
- ½ medium diced yellow onions
- 8g/2 teaspoons of seasoned salt
- 3 cloves of minced garlic

DIRECTIONS

1. Spray the bottom of a 5-quart slow cooker with a small amount of nonstick cooking spray.
2. Now, put in the capsicums, onion, garlic, potatoes, seasoned salt, butter, and paprika.
3. Top with some olive oil before mixing to combine.
4. Allow cooking on a covered slow cooker either on the high setting which should take 2-3 hours or on the low setting that takes roughly 4-5 to cook the potatoes.
5. Remember that your cooking time will be relative to the type of slow cooker you have and the sizes of the potato dices. Therefore, be sure to check for readiness before the said time.
6. Add some salt and pepper once cooked and serve.

Slower Cooker Healthy Banana Bread

Time: 4 hours 5 minutes | Servings 6
Kcal 296, Carbs 64.9g/2.26oz, Fats 2.1g/0.08oz, Proteins 5.5g/0.19oz, Fiber 1.9g/0.06oz

INGREDIENTS

- ◆ 64g/½ a cup of diced chocolate
- ◆ 3 large ripe bananas
- ◆ 4 large eggs
- ◆ 50g/1.8oz of honey
- ◆ 6g/1½ teaspoons of vanilla extract
- ◆ 128g/1 cup of oats
- ◆ Grated zest of ½ orange
- ◆ 250ml/1 cup of water
- ◆ 2g/½ a teaspoon of Bicarbonate of soda
- ◆ 4g/1 teaspoon of ground cinnamon
- ◆ A pinch of ground nutmeg

1. Begin by peeling and slicing the bananas into a mixing bowl before mashing using a fork.

2. Now add in water, nutmeg, honey, bicarbonate soda, water, cinnamon, chocolate, eggs, orange zest, and vanilla extract in another bowl. Stir everything together till even.

3. Scoop the mixture into your slow cooker before setting the cooker to high which should cook for roughly 3 hours. However, if you want a softer consistency, cook under the low setting which should take a bit longer.

4. Be sure to stir occasionally to prevent the mixture from sticking on the sides of the cooker.

5. Bring the oven to a temperature of 93°C/200°F.

6. Once the banana bread is cooked, cover with coconut before cooking in the oven till the top is caramelized.

7. Serve immediately with the mashed banana atop.

Lunch Recipes

Slow Cooker Meatballs

Time: 6 hours | Servings 5
Kcal 260, Carbs 21g/0.74oz, Fats 5g/0.17oz, Proteins 29g/1.02oz, Fiber 5g/0.17oz

INGREDIENTS

- ◆ Cooking spray
- ◆ 15ml/1 teaspoon of rapeseed oil
- ◆ 1 clove of minced garlic
- ◆ 1 finely chopped onions
- ◆ A pinch of paprika
- ◆ 2 finely chopped carrots
- ◆ 68g/4 teaspoons of porridge oats
- ◆ 2 finely chopped celery sticks
- ◆ 400g/14oz of lean minced turkey
- ◆ 2 garlic cloves thinly sliced
- ◆ 8g/2 teaspoons of chopped parsley
- ◆ 500g/17oz carton of tomato passata

DIRECTIONS

1. Bring a nonstick frying pan to heat under medium temperature before adding in the 2 cloves of sliced garlic, celery, onion, and carrots.

2. Quickly fry the ingredients before pouring in the passata and parsley then toss to mix everything well then move everything to the slow cooker.

3. To prepare the meatballs, add the minced turkey into a large mixing bowl.

4. Now, add in the paprika, oats, minced garlic, and black pepper before tossing and mixing up the ingredients with your hands.

5. Make 20 equal lumps out of the meatball mixture then make round meatballs from each lump mixture.

6. Gently coat a nonstick cooking pan with cooking spray and cook the ingredients allowing the meatballs to cook till slightly brown.

7. Once done, put the meatballs to the tomato base in the slow cooker and let them cook for 5 hours.

8. Serve with some pasta or green salad of your choice.

The Slow Cooker Beef and Beer

Time: 6 hours | Serves 8
Kcal 345, Carbs 18g/0.63oz, Fats 13g/0.46oz, Proteins 20g/0.71oz, Fiber 5g/0.18oz

INGREDIENTS

- 230g/8oz of button mushrooms each halved
- 15ml/1 tablespoon of canola oil
- 4 bay leaves
- 1.3kg/3oz of chuck roast
- 15ml/1 tablespoon of Worcestershire sauce
- Black pepper and salt
- 500ml/2 cups of low sodium beef stock
- 30ml/2 tablespoons of red wine vinegar
- 1 can of dark beer of your choice
- 5 sliced yellow onions

DIRECTIONS

1. Bring the oil to heat in a medium to a large-sized skillet over medium temperatures.

2. Sprinkle salt and pepper over the chuck for seasoning before going to the next step.

3. Now, put the beef in the preheated pan and sear till nice and brown for around 10 minutes.

4. Once done, remove the cooked beef before adding in beer, onions, and vinegar to the pan and cook for a few minutes. Be sure to scrape off any remnants that may cling to the bottom of the pan.

5. Put the browned beef at the bottom of your cooker before adding in the onion-beer mixture atop.

6. Throw in the bay leaves, Worcestershire sauce, and the stock. The liquid should cover the beef, if not add more beer.

7. Allow cooking for 6 hours on the low settings or 4 hours in the high setting. The cooking time is relative to the type of slow cooker you are using.

8. Put the mushrooms in the cooker in the last hour of your cooking to avoid overcooking them.

9. Remove the bay leaves before serving with some veggies and a sauce of your choice.

Slow Cooker Basque Chicken

Time: 4 hours 20 minutes | Servings 4
Kcal 370, Carbs 18g/0.63oz, Fats 20g/0.7oz, Proteins 16g/0.56oz, Fiber 2g/0.07oz

INGREDIENTS

- 200g/4 cups of baby spinach
- 15ml/1 tablespoon of olive oil
- 2 bay leaves
- 4 bone-in, skin-on chicken breast
- 2g/½ a teaspoon of cumin
- Black pepper and salt
- 4g/1 teaspoon of smoked paprika
- 1 link of sliced Spanish chorizo
- 4g/1 teaspoon of smoked paprika
- 1 can/12oz of black beer of your choice
- 8 cloves of peeled garlic
- 375ml/1½ cups of low sodium chicken stock
- 1 chopped red bell pepper
- 30ml/2 tablespoons of red wine vinegar
- 1 quartered large onion

DIRECTIONS

1. Bring the oil to heat in a good-sized frying pan over medium to high temperatures briefly.

2. Sprinkle the chicken breasts with pepper and salt to the season before putting them on the skillet and brown both sides for around 7 minutes.

3. Now, put in the chorizo and cook for an additional 2 minutes till they brown as well.

4. Move the cooked meat into the slow cooker.

5. In the skillet, pour the beer and scrape off any remnants that may stick at the bottom before adding the beer to the slow cooker.

6. Top with the onions, bell pepper, vinegar, stock, cumin, paprika, bay leaves, and garlic then Cook for 4 hours.

7. Put in the spinach 10 minutes before switching off the slow cooker which is enough time for warming and cooking in the braising liquid.

8. Remove the bay leaves before serving, taste, and adjust the seasoning accordingly.

9. Now serve in bowls and top with the braising liquid.

Slow Cooker Beef and Broccoli

Time: 3 hours 20 minutes | Servings 3
Kcal 281, Carbs 2g/0.07oz, Fats 29g/1oz, Protein 4g/0.14oz, Fiber 4g/0.14oz

INGREDIENTS

- 17g/1 tablespoon of cornstarch
- 450g/16oz sliced flank steak
- 250ml/1 cup of beef stock
- 2 broccoli crowns sliced into florets
- 5ml/1 teaspoon of honey
- 15ml/1 tablespoon of rice vinegar
- 125ml/ ½ a cup of soy sauce
- 4g/1 teaspoon of Sriracha
- 17g/1 tablespoon of brown sugar
- 2 cloves of minced garlic
- 8g/2 teaspoons of grated ginger

DIRECTIONS

1. Put the flank steak and broccoli florets into the slow cooker.

2. Using a small mixing bowl, add in the soy sauce, brown sugar, rice vinegar, chili flakes, Sriracha, garlic, grated ginger, and honey. Stir to mix everything up.

3. Now empty the contents of the bowl into the slow cooker and mix well with the broccoli and steak.

4. Add in the beef stock and mix further.

5. Turn your slow cooker to the Low settings and cook for 2 hours.

6. Mix the cornstarch with 60ml/¼ cup of water to form a slurry then pour it into the slow cooker in the last 30 minutes.

7. Serve with some rice and top with sesame seeds if you so wish.

Slow-Cooker on Classic French Pot Roast

Time: 4 hours 20 minutes | Servings 4
Kcal 500, Carbs 77g/2.17oz, Fats 15g/0.53oz, Proteins 20g/0.72oz, Fiber 16g/0.56oz

INGREDIENTS

- 128g/1 cup of frozen peas
- 2 strips of bacon (striped)
- 230g/½ lb. of mushrooms
- 32g/¼ cup of flour
- 250g/2 cups of frozen pearl onions
- Black pepper and salt
- 2 bay leaves
- 900g/2 lbs. chuck roast with excess fat removed
- 34g/2 tablespoons of tomato paste
- ½ a bottle of dry red wine
- 500g/2 cups of low sodium beef broth

DIRECTIONS

1. Over a medium to high heat, preheat a medium to a large skillet or sauté pan.
2. Put in the bacon strips and cook till all the fat is rendered or till it gets nice and crisp.
3. Once done, remove the bacon from the pan before draining using paper towels. Put the bacon aside and let the pan continue heating.
4. Now, mix salt, pepper, and the flour in a sealable plastic bag.
5. Put the beef pieces into the flour mixture in batches then shake everything up to coat the beef pieces evenly.
6. Shake off any excess flour from the meat pieces before putting them in the pan. Cook till both sides are nice and brown.
7. Move the browned beef from the pan to the slow cooker.
8. Pour 1 cup of wine into the pan and scrape off any beef remnants from the pan and pour over the beef in the slow cooker.
9. Top with the bay leaves, the remainder of the wine, tomato sauce, and bacon pieces.
10. Set your slow cooker to high and allow the beef to cook for 4 hours till the beef tenders up.
11. 20 minutes out of your cooking time, add in the mushrooms and pearl onions.
12. Add the peas and simmer for a few minutes right before serving.
13. Remove the bay leaves and serve with some mashed potatoes on the side.

Slow Cooker Lamb Tagine

Time: 4 hours 10 minutes | Servings 8
Kcal 440, Carbs 40g/2.04oz, Fats 7g/0.25oz, Proteins 44g/2.49oz, Fiber 4g/0.14oz

INGREDIENTS

- Chopped cilantro
- 15ml/1 tablespoon of olive oil
- 250g/2 cups of cooked couscous
- 900g/2 lbs. of lamb stewing meat
- ¼ golden raisins
- Black pepper and salt
- 1 can of 425g/15oz of chickpeas
- 250ml/2 cups of low-sodium chicken stock
- 1g/¼ a teaspoon of cayenne
- 2 quartered large onions
- 1 stick cinnamon
- 4 peeled and chopped carrots
- 4g/1 teaspoon of cumin
- 3 seeded and chopped Roma tomatoes

- 6 cloves of peeled garlic
- 17g/1 tablespoon of minced fresh ginger

DIRECTIONS

1. In a large skillet, bring the oil to heat up under medium to high temperatures.
2. Sprinkle the lamb with some pepper and salt before putting them in the pan. Allow cooking for 7 minutes till the meat is browned on both sides.
3. Move the lamb to a slow cooker before pouring some stock in the pan and scraping off any lamb remnants.
4. Pour the liquid into the slow cooker before topping with the tomatoes, garlic, ginger, cumin, onions, cayenne, and cinnamon.
5. Cook the mixture on your slow cooker under the high settings for 4 hours or 8 hours under the low setting till the lamb is tender and falls apart.
6. Stir in the raisins and chickpeas 20 minutes before time to avoid overcooking.
7. Remove the cinnamon sticks before tasting and adjusting the seasoning accordingly.
8. To serve, put the tagine over the couscous and spread some freshly chopped cilantro leaves atop.

Slow Cooker Lasagne

Time: 4 hours 15 minutes | Servings 4
Kcal 448, Carbs 46g/1.62oz, Fats 12g/0.42oz, Proteins 33g/1.16oz, Fiber 9g/0.31oz

INGREDIENTS

- 105g/3.7oz whole-wheat lasagne sheet
- 10ml/2 teaspoons of rapeseed oil
- 17g/1 tablespoon of fresh thyme leaves
- 2 finely chopped onions
- 15ml/1 tablespoon of balsamic vinegar
- 4 finely chopped celery sticks

For the sauce

- 15g/0.53 finely grated parmesan
- 400ml/⅔ cup of whole milk
- Nutmeg
- 50g/1.7oz of wholemeal flour
- 1 bay leaf

- 8g/2 teaspoons of vegetable bouillon
- 320g/4 finely chopped carrots
- 30ml/2 tablespoons of tomato puree
- 2 cloves of chopped garlic
- 400g/14oz can of chopped tomatoes
- 400g/14oz of lean 5% fat minced beef

DIRECTIONS

1. Bring the oil to heat up in a medium to a large skillet over medium temperature. Throw in the celery, onions, garlic, and carrots and allow them to fry for 10 minutes.

2. Put in the meat breaking it down using a spatula and stir frequently till it browns evenly.

3. Add in the tomato puree, bouillon, thyme, vinegar, black pepper, and tomatoes with a quarter the water can.

4. Stir and allow the mixture to cook for an additional 5 minutes.

5. Now scoop half of the mince and put at the bottom of the slow cooker. Cover with half the lasagne ensuring it covers as much of the mince as possible.

6. Scoop the remaining mince and put atop the lasagne layer then cover with the remainder of the lasagne pieces.

7. Allow everything to cook under the low setting in your slow cooker.

8. To prepare the sauce, pour the milk, flour, nutmeg, and the bay leaf into a skillet and cook on a stovetop.

9. Stir the mixture continuously till you achieve a thick consistency.

10. Cook for a few minutes more before removing the bay leaves and stirring in the cheese.

11. Pour the sauce atop the contents on the slow cooker and spread the sauce out evenly.

12. Allow everything to cook together for 3 hours until the meat gets tender.

13. Once done, switch off the slow cooker and let the food sit for 10 minutes before serving with some salad.

Slow Cooker Pork Fillets with Apples

Time: 4 hours 15 minutes | Servings 4
Kcal 344, Carbs 18g/0.63oz, Fats 14g/0.49oz, Proteins 33g/1.16oz, Fiber 5g/0.17oz

INGREDIENTS

- 34g/1 tablespoons of half-fat crème fraiche
- 7ml/½ tablespoon of rapeseed oil
- 4 finely sliced sage leaves
- 500g/17oz of pork fillets sliced into medallions
- 17g/1 teaspoon of Dijon Mustard
- 1 finely chopped medium onion
- 150ml/½ a cup of chicken stock
- 3 eating apples

1. Bring the oil to heat up on a medium nonstick skillet over medium heat.
2. Quickly fry the medallions on both sides for 2 minutes till they get a light color.
3. Now throw in the onions and allow them to fry for a few minutes before adding in the mustard and chicken stock to the mixture.
4. Transfer the pork mixture and fluid into the slow cooker.
5. Quarter the apples then remove the core before putting them into the pot together with the sage.
6. Sprinkle some black pepper to taste before turning the slow cooker into the low setting and cook for 4 hours.
7. Finish by stirring in the crème fraiche.

The Slow Cooker Chicken Casserole

Time: 4 hours 20 minutes | Servings 4
Kcal 382, Carbs 30g/1.05oz, Fats 9g/0.32oz, Proteins 41g/1.44oz, Fiber 6g/0.21oz

INGREDIENTS

- 2 bay leaves
- Knob of butter
- 12g/3 teaspoons of Dijon mustard
- 7ml/½ a tablespoon of rapeseed oil
- 500ml/2 cups of low-chicken stock
- 1 large finely chopped onion
- 15g/0.53oz of dried porcini mushrooms soaked in 50ml/4 tablespoon of water
- 25g/1½ tablespoons of flour
- 2 diced carrots
- 650g/23oz of skinless, boneless chicken thigh fillets
- 2 diced celery sticks
- 3 cloves of crushed garlic
- 400g/14oz of halved baby new potatoes

1. Using a large skillet, bring the knob of oil and ½ tablespoon of rapeseed oil to heat over medium to high temperatures.
2. Put in the finely chopped onion and allow them to cook until caramelized for roughly 10 minutes.
3. Using a mixing bowl, combine the salt, flour, butter, and the chicken thigh fillets and toss everything together.
4. Once the onions are nice and caramelized, put in the crushed garlic and the chicken thigh fillets and cook for 5 minutes or until the fillets start browning on both sides.
5. Move everything to the slow cooker before putting in the baby potatoes carrots, celery, mushrooms, porcini mushrooms with the soaking liquid, bay leaves, chicken stock, and Dijon mustard sparing some for serving.
6. Stir, cover, and allow cooking for 4 hours under the high settings or 7 hours under the low settings on the slow cooker.
7. Once cooked, discard the bay leaves before serving with some Dijon mustard on the side.

Slow Cooker Shepherd's Pie

Time: 1 hour 5 minutes | Servings 4
Kcal 438, Carbs 57g/2oz, Fats 10g/0.35oz, Proteins 23g/0.81oz, Fiber 11g/0.39oz

INGREDIENTS

- 34g/2 tablespoons of half-fat crème fraiche
- 15ml/1 tablespoon of olive oil
- 250g/8.8oz of peeled sweet potatoes, sliced into chunks
- 1 finely chopped onion
- 5ml/1 teaspoon of Worcestershire sauce
- 4 thyme sprigs
- 400g/12oz can lentils
- 2 finely chopped carrots
- 15ml/1 tablespoon of tomato puree
- 250g/8.8oz of lean 10% minced lamb
- 17g/1 tablespoon of plain flour
- 650g/22oz of peeled potatoes and cut into chunks

DIRECTIONS

1. In a large frying pan, bring the oil to heat over medium heat.
2. Put in the thyme sprigs and onions then cook for 3 minutes before putting in the carrots and cooking them together till the veggies begin to brown.
3. Now put in the minced lamb and cook until all the pink color is no more.
4. Add in the flour and mix well before allowing everything to cook together for another 2 minutes.
5. Toss in the lentils and tomato puree before topping with some black pepper and Worcestershire sauce.
6. If the mixture is still too dry add some water and stir.
7. Scrape and move everything into the slow cooker.
8. As the mince mixture cooks, put both potatoes in simmering water and allow them to cook until they are cooked through for roughly 12 minutes.
9. Drain the excess water and carefully mash the potatoes with crème fraiche.
10. Scoop the topping and add on top of the mince mixture and allow everything to cook in the slow cooker together.

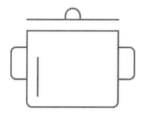

Dinner Recipes

The Slow Cooker Chicken Tikka Masala

Time: 4 hours 50 minutes | Servings 4
Kcal 599, Carbs 17g/0.6oz, Fats 43g/1.5oz, Proteins 33g/1.16oz, Fiber 4g/0.14oz

INGREDIENTS

- Cooked basmati rice for serving
- 10 skinless, boneless chicken thighs cut into 3 chunks
- A handful of chopped coriander leaves
- 30ml/2 tablespoons of rapeseed oil
- 100ml/ ¾ cup of double cream
- 1 chopped large onion
- 5 cardamom pods
- 2 crushed cloves of garlic
- 1 cinnamon stick
- 1 chopped thumb-sized ginger
- 17g/1 tablespoon of light brown soft sugar
- 45ml/3 tablespoons of tikka curry paste
- 15ml/1 tablespoon malt vinegar
- 500ml/1 cup of passata
- 15ml/1 tablespoon of tomato puree

DIRECTIONS

1. Season the chicken with some salt and pepper.
2. Bring the oil to heat in a large pan over medium temperatures. Once hot enough, put in the seasoned chicken thigh pieces. Remember to give each piece of chicken enough space in the pan. Cook in batches.
3. Allow cooking in the pan till the chicken browns evenly on both sides before moving them to the slow cooker.
4. Now put the garlic, onion, and ginger on the pan and allow cooking for 2 minutes till they get nice and soft.
5. Pour some water in the pan and scrape off any remnants then pour the liquid over the chicken in the slow cooker.
6. Put every other ingredient but the coriander and cream in the slow cooker and adjust the seasoning accordingly.
7. Allow cooking for 5 hours using the low setting in the slow cooker or for 4 hours using the high setting.
8. Now, add in the cream adjusting the salt, sugar, or vinegar accordingly before cooking for an additional 15 minutes till hot.
9. Serve in between bowl and top with some coriander.
10. Enjoy with some basmati rice on the side.

Slow Cooker Beef Stew

Time: 4 hours 20 minutes | Servings 4
Kcal 473, Carbs 10g/0.35oz, Fats 25g/0.88oz, Proteins 48g/1.7oz, Fiber 4g/0.14oz

INGREDIENTS

- Buttery mash for serving
- 1 chopped onion
- Small bunch of chopped parsley
- 2 finely chopped celery sticks
- 8g/2 teaspoons of cornflour
- 30ml/2 tablespoon of rapeseed oil
- 900g/30oz of diced beef for braising
- 3 carrots cut into small chunks
- 2 beef stock cubes
- 2 bay leaves
- 30ml/2 tablespoons of Worcestershire sauce
- ½ a pack of thyme
- 30ml/2 tablespoons of tomato puree

DIRECTIONS

1. Bring 15ml/1 tablespoon of oil to heat up in a skillet before adding in the celery and onions. Allow cooking until they are nice and soft.
2. Add in the thyme, bay, and carrots then fry for 2 more minutes.
3. Pour in the tomato puree Worcestershire sauce, 600ml/1½ cups of boiling water then stir and transfer everything into the slow cooker.
4. Add in the crumbled stock cubes and adjust the pepper seasoning.
5. Using the remainder of the oil, fry the beef in the frying pan until it is nice and brown before transferring each piece to the slow cooker.
6. Allow cooking for 8 hours on the low settings or 4 hours in high settings.
7. To thicken the gravy, mix some cold water with the cornstarch to a paste then mix in 30ml/2 tablespoons of the liquid from the slow cooker.
8. Now, pour back the paste into the slow cooker and allow cooking for 15 minutes on the high settings
9. Serve and enjoy with some mash on the side.

Slow Cooker Chilli Con Carne

Time: 6 hours 25 minutes | Servings 6
Kcal 281, Carbs 18g/0.63oz, Fats 13g/0.46oz, Proteins 19g/0.67oz, Fiber 6g/0.21oz

INGREDIENTS

- Tortilla chips
- 45ml/3 tablespoons of olive oil
- 4 small square dark chocolate
- 500g/17oz mince beef
- 800g/28oz can of drained black beans
- 1 finely chopped onion
- 400ml/1½ cup of beef stock
- 1 finely chopped celery stick
- 400g/14oz can of chopped tomatoes
- 1 thickly sliced red bell pepper
- 45ml/3 tablespoons of chipotle chili paste
- 2 finely grated garlic cloves
- 45ml/3 tablespoons of tomato puree
- 8g/2 teaspoons of ground cumin
- 8g/2 teaspoons of dried oregano
- 4g/1 teaspoon of smoked paprika

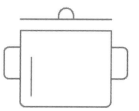

DIRECTIONS

1. Bring 20ml/1½ tablespoons of oil to heat in a large frying pan over high temperature.
2. Put in the minced beef and cook until they brown evenly for 10 minutes before moving to the slow cooker.
3. Using the remainder of the oil, fry the pepper, celery, and onions till they get nice and tender.
4. Now, top with the paprika, cumin, and garlic then cook for an additional minute or two before transferring to the slow cooker.
5. Mix in the tomato puree, oregano, chipotle, tomatoes, and stock.
6. Allow cooking for 6 to 8 hours depending on the setting you choose on the cooker.
7. During the last 30 minutes of your cooking add in the chocolate pieces and beans.
8. Serve with a dollop of sour cream and tortilla chips.

Slow Cooker Pork Loin

Time: 5 hours 30 minutes | Servings 5
Kcal 597, Carbs 9g/0.3oz, Fats 41g/1.44oz, Proteins 42g/1.48oz, Fiber 4g/0.14oz

INGREDIENTS

- 15ml/1 tablespoon of Dijon mustard
- 6g/1½ teaspoons of fennel seeds
- 15ml/1 tablespoon of honey
- 3 sprigs of fresh thyme
- 250ml/1 cup of pork stock
- 2 cloves of garlic
- 150ml/½ a cup of white wine
- 30ml/2 tablespoons of rapeseed oil
- 2 eating apple wedges
- 1.8kg/4 lbs. of pork loin with skin removed and fat well scored
- 300g/10oz of shallots
- 1 small celeriac quartered and peeled

DIRECTIONS

1. Using a pestle and mortar, crush the garlic, thyme leaves, and fennel seeds.
2. Put in some oil and water then make a rough paste out of the mixture.
3. Coat the paste over the pork before covering and allow to chill to up to 24 hours.
4. Pour a cup of boiling water over the shallots to make them easy to peel.
5. Begin by removing the roots before papery skin.
6. Now bring the remainder of the oil to heat in a large frying pan over medium heat.
7. Quickly fry the shallots for a few minutes till nice and brown then transfer them to the slow cooker.
8. Season the apples and celeriac then add them to the slow cooker and toss everything to mix.
9. On the frying pan, brown the pork evenly on all sides not forgetting the ends.
10. Put the browned pork on top of the veggies having the fat side up.
11. Boil the wine in the frying pan, scraping off any tasty bits, pour in the honey stock and mustard, and allow to boil for a few minutes before transferring the liquid in the slow cooker.
12. Allow cooking in the slow cooker for 4 to 6 hours tossing the pork and veggies halfway through the cooking.
13. When done, remove the pork from the cooker and wrap it with pork then let sit for 10 minutes before slicing to serve with the veggies and roast potatoes on the side.

Slow Cooker Paella

Time 2 hours 40 minutes | Servings 2
Kcal 517, Carbs 46g/1.6oz, Fats 21g/0.74oz, Proteins 31g/1.09oz, Fiber 5g/0.17oz

INGREDIENTS

- Crusty bread and lemon wedges for serving
- 30ml/2 tablespoons of olive oil
- Small bunch of finely chopped parsley
- 4 thickly sliced pieces of boneless and skinless chicken slices
- 200g/7oz of fresh or frozen king prawns
- 240g/8oz of sliced chorizo rings
- 150g/5oz of frozen peas
- 1 sliced onion
- 400ml/1½ cups of chicken stock
- 2 cloves of crushed garlic
- 400g/14oz of canned chopped tomatoes
- 8g/1 teaspoon of sweet smoked paprika
- 300g/10oz paella rice
- A pinch of saffron
- 150ml/½ a cup of white wine

1. Bring a pan to heat under medium temperatures. Add in the oil and cook the chorizo and chicken then fry for 10 minutes till nice and golden.
2. Transfer the chicken to the Slow cooker then add the onions to the pan and cook till they are tender.
3. Add in the saffron, garlic, and paprika then fry for 2 minutes.
4. Top up with some wine and allow to simmer till reduced by half.
5. Now transfer everything into the slow cooker together with the tomatoes, stock, and rice.
6. Allow everything to cook up for 1½ hours before adding in the peas and prawns and cook for an additional 30 minutes or more depending on the readiness of the rice.
7. Spread atop the parsley and serve with the crusty bread and lemon wedges on the side.

Slow Cooker Mushroom Risotto

Time: 1 hour 30 minutes | Servings 4
Kcal 346, Carbs 67g/2.3oz, Fats 3g/0.09oz, Proteins 10g/0.34oz, Fiber 5g/0.17oz

INGREDIENTS

- Grated vegetarian parmesan cheese
- 1 finely chopped onion
- A small bunch of finely chopped parsley
- 15ml/1 teaspoon of olive oil
- 300g/10oz of whole grain rice
- 1L/4 cups of vegetable stock
- 250g/8oz of sliced chestnut mushrooms
- 50g/1.7oz of porcini

DIRECTIONS

1. Heat the oil in a nonstick frying pan and add in the onions. Allow cooking for 10 minutes with a splash of water.

2. Now throw in the mushroom slices and toss around till they start getting tender and release their fluids.

3. Put the stock in the saucepan and throw in the porcini letting them simmer and soak for some time.

4. Transfer the mushrooms and onions into the slow cooker adding the rice and stir well.

5. Pour the stock and porcini atop the leaving any residue in the saucepan.

6. Using the high setting on the slow cooker, allow cooking for 3 hours. Be sure to stir halfway through the cooking.

7. If the rice needs more cooking top up some more stock.

8. Spread some parsley and serve with some parmesan.

Slow Cooker Ham with Sticky Ginger Glaze

Time: 7 hours 20 minutes | Servings 7
Kcal 363, Carbs 31g/1.09oz, Fats 14g/0.49oz, Proteins 27g/0.95oz, Fiber 1g/0.03oz

INGREDIENTS

- 51g/3 tablespoons of ginger preserve
- 1 thickly sliced onion
- 17g/1 tablespoons of English mustard
- 10 cloves
- 1.5L/6 cups of ginger beer
- 1.3kg/45oz medium gammon joint

DIRECTIONS

1. Begin by throwing in 9 cloves and the onion at the base of the slow cooking appliance before nestling in the gammon joint.
2. Now pour in the ginger beer and cook in the slow cooker for 7 hours under the low settings till the gammon tenders up but retains its shape.
3. At this stage, bring the oven to a temperature of 93°C/200°F.
4. Carefully skin the gammon leaving a layer of fat. In diamond shapes, score the fat using a knife. Be sure you don't cut into the meat.
5. Stud the center of the diamonds with cloves.
6. Now, mix the ginger preserve with the mustard before brushing it over the gammon.
7. Cook in the oven for 20 minutes or till the gammon is brown and sticky.

Slow Cooker Rice Pudding

Time: 2 hours 50 minutes | Servings 6
Kcal 200, Carbs 32g/1.13oz, Fats 4g/0.14oz, Proteins 8g/0.28oz, Fiber 1g/0.03oz

INGREDIENTS

- 15ml/1 tablespoon of honey
- 4g/1 teaspoon of butter
- Cinnamon or nutmeg
- 1L/4 cups of semi-skimmed milk
- 200g/7oz wholegrain rice

DIRECTIONS

1. Grease the slow cooker using the butter at the bottom and half way along the sides.
2. Bring the milk to simmer under medium temperatures before adding in the pudding rice.
3. Mix the rice well with the hot milk before tipping everything into the pre-greased slow cooker.
4. Put in a grating of cinnamon or nutmeg depending on your preference and stir.
5. Turn the high setting on, and allow cooking in the slow cooker for 2½ hours. Be sure to stir at least once during the cooking period.
6. Once done, serve with some honey or fruit on the side of you so wish.
7. Enjoy!

Aubergine and Chickpea Stew

Time: 8 hours 15 minutes | Servings 6
Kcal 266, Carbs 27g/0.95oz, Fats 10g/0.3oz, Proteins 11g/0.39oz, Fiber 12g/0.42oz

INGREDIENTS

- Pitta bread
- 200g/7oz drained and soaked chickpeas
- 50g/1.7oz toasted pine nuts
- 30ml/2 tablespoons of extra virgin olive oil
- 1 juiced lemon
- 2 finely sliced onions
- 800g/28oz can of chopped tomatoes
- 6 cloves of crushed garlic
- 3 medium sliced aubergines
- 17g/1 tablespoon of baharat
- Finely chopped bunch of flat-leafed parsley

DIRECTIONS

1. Begin by draining the chickpeas before boiling in salted water in a pan for 10 minutes before draining again.
2. Using a medium pan, bring the oil to heat up under medium temperature and cook the onions for 10 minutes till they are nice and tender.
3. Toss in the baharat, cinnamon, and garlic then proceed to cook for an additional minute till nice and fragrant.
4. Pour the mixture into the slow cooker then add in the chickpeas, aubergines, chopped parsley, a can of water, and finally tomatoes.
5. Allow cooking under the high setting for 2 hours then switch to low and cook for an additional 6 hours till the mixture reduces significantly and the aubergines and chickpeas are tender.
6. Mix the lemon juice in, then add the nuts.
7. Top with the olive oil before serving with the pitta bread.

Slow Cooked Leg of Lamb

Time: 7 hours 50 minutes | Servings 6
Kcal 743, Carbs 14g/0.49oz, Fats 41g/1.44oz, Proteins 73g/2.6oz, Fiber 3g/0.1oz

INGREDIENTS

- ♦ Thyme sprigs
- ♦ 3kg/6 lbs. 8oz leg of lamb
- ♦ 34g/2 tablespoons of Armagnac
- ♦ 4 sliced onions
- ♦ 300ml/1¼ cups of stock
- ♦ 8 peeled cloves of garlic
- ♦ 300ml/1¼ cups of white wine
- ♦ 4 quartered lengthwise carrots

DIRECTIONS

1. Bring the oven to a temperature of 48°C/120°F.
2. Season the lamb and brown every side evenly using a large enough casserole with a lid. Be sure to brown completely since browning won't happen during cooking.
3. Allow cooking for 10 minutes pouring any unwanted fat that will collect at the bottom of the pan.
4. Once done, add in the vegetables followed by the stock and then wine.
5. Season the mixture before boiling. Now transfer everything into the slow cooker and cook under the low setting for 7 hours.
6. Once done, strain the stew in a separate bowl before blotting the fat with a paper towel.
7. Pour the sauce into a pan and allow it to boil till it reduces by a half.
8. By this time the sauce will be thick and flavor-rich vegetarian, adjust the seasoning, and serve with the lamb.

Vegetarian Recipes

. . . .

Slow Cooker Ratatouille

Time: 6 hours 30 minutes | Servings 6
Kcal 162, Carbs 17g/0.6oz, Fats 5g/0.17oz, Proteins 6g/0.21oz, Fiber 11g/0.38oz

INGREDIENTS

- Sourdough for serving
- 30ml/2 tablespoons of olive oil
- 4g/1 teaspoon of brown sugar
- 1 sliced red onion
- 15ml/1 tablespoon of red wine vinegar
- 2 garlic cloves
- 400g/14oz can of plum tomatoes
- 2 large and sliced aubergines
- A few thyme sprigs
- 3 coarsely chopped courgettes
- A small batch of roughly chopped basil
- 3 mixed and chopped peppers
- 6 roughly chopped ripe tomatoes
- 15ml/1 tablespoon of tomato puree

DIRECTIONS

1. Bring the oil to heat up in a large skillet before adding in the chopped onions and allowing them to cook till they get nice and translucent.
2. Put in the garlic and fry for an additional minute.
3. Reduce the heat to medium before adding in the aubergines then go ahead and fry for 5 minutes till they turn brown.
4. Now toss in pepper and courgettes and fry for 5 more minutes till they get soft.
5. Throw in the herbs, tomato puree, canned tomatoes, fresh tomato pieces, sugar, vinegar, and a pinch of salt then bring everything to boil.
6. Move the entire batch to the slow cooker and allow to cook under low setting for 5 to 6 hours till the sauce is nice and thick.
7. Garnish with some basil before serving with the sourdough.

Slow-Cooker Vegetable Lasagne

Time: 3 hours 30 minutes | Servings 4
Kcal 325, Carbs 36g/1.27oz, Fats 11g/0.39oz, Proteins 15g/0.53oz, Fiber 11g/0.39oz

INGREDIENTS

- 125g/4.4oz of vegetarian buffalo mozzarella
- 15ml/1 tablespoon of rapeseed oil
- 6 whole wheat lasagne sheets
- 2 sliced onions
- 1 large aubergine sliced lengthwise
- 2 large chopped garlic cloves
- 15g/0.5oz of freshly chopped basil
- 2 large diced courgettes
- 8g/2 tablespoons of vegetable bouillon
- 1 yellow and 1 red pepper deseeded and coarsely chopped
- 30ml/2 tablespoons of tomato puree
- 400g/14oz of chopped tomatoes

DIRECTIONS

1. Bring the rapeseed oil to heat up in a large nonstick pan before throwing in the garlic. Allow cooking for 5 minutes till they get soft.

2. Now, add in the capsicum, tomato puree, courgettes, vegetable bouillon, and chopped basil.

3. Cover and let everything cook up. Don't add any liquid since the required moisture will come from the vegetables.

4. Slice into half one aubergine and lay at the base of the slow cooking appliance then layer atop with 3 lasagne sheets.

5. Layer on top of the lasagne sheets ⅓ of the ratatouille mixture and top with the remainder of the aubergine slices, 3 lasagne sheets, and finally the last batch of the ratatouille mixture atop.

6. Allow cooking in the slow cooker till the veggies and pasta get tender for roughly 2½ to 3 hours.

7. Sprinkle atop the buffalo mozzarella cheese and cook for 10 more minutes till all the cheese has melted.

8. Spread some basil on top and serve!

Slow Cooker Vegetable Stew with Cheddar Dumplings

Time: 6 hours 20 minutes | Servings 6
Kcal 554, Carbs 40g/1.4oz, Fats 33g/1.16oz, Proteins 18g/0.63oz, Fiber 13g/0.46oz

INGREDIENTS

- Small bunch of finely chopped parsley
- 30ml/2 tablespoons of olive oil
- 200g/7oz of spinach
- 200g/7oz of baby carrots
- 200g/7oz of bread beans
- 3 leeks chopped coarsely
- 15ml/1 tablespoon of whole grain mustard
- 3 cloves of crushed garlic

For the dumplings

- Small bunch of finely chopped parsley
- 100g/3½oz of self-rising flour
- 100g/3½oz of mature cheddar
- 50g/1.7oz of vegetarian suet

- 250ml/1 cup of crème fraiche
- 52g/3 tablespoons of plain flour
- 4 thyme rosemary
- 400ml/2 cups of vegetable stock
- 1 bay leaf
- 2 courgettes chopped coarsely
- 800g/28oz drained and rinsed cannellini beans

DIRECTIONS

1. Bring 1 tablespoon of oil to heat up in a frying pan. Fry the carrots for 5 minutes till golden before putting them in the slow cooker.
2. Using the remainder of the oil, fry the leeks with some salt until they get soft for approximately 5 minutes.
3. Throw in the garlic and add in the flour.
4. Carefully, pour in the stock as you stir continuously till all the flour has dissolved and there are no more lumps.
5. Allow the mixture to boil then toss everything into the slow cooker.
6. Now put in the courgettes, herbs, and beans before pouring in water to cover the veggies. Cook for 4 hours using the low setting on your slow cooker.
7. Meanwhile, make the dumplings by mixing the flour, suet, and butter in a mixing bowl and mixing until everything is well balanced and distributed.
8. Add in the parsley, some salt, and black pepper before adding in 5 tablespoons of water and mix thoroughly to achieve a slightly sticky dough.
9. Now divide the dough into 6 and roll to make round balls.
10. In the last 1 or 2 hours, add in the Crème Fraiche, spinach, broad beans, and mustard to the slow cooker and turn it to the high setting.
11. Put the dumplings over the stew and let them cook till they double in size and get firm.
12. Sprinkle with some parsley when done and serve.

Slow Cooker Spiced Root and Lentil Casserole

Time: 5 hours 50 minutes | Servings 4
Kcal 333, Carbs 44g/1.55oz, Fats 9g/0.32oz, Proteins 13g/0.46oz, Fiber 15g/0.53oz

INGREDIENTS

- Lemon juice for serving
- 15ml/2 tablespoons of olive oil
- 2 bay leaves
- 1 finely chopped onion
- 600ml/2¼ cups of hot vegan vegetable stock
- 5 medium coarsely chopped parsnip
- 150g/5oz of rinsed red lentils
- 3 peeled and chopped carrots
- 17g/1 tablespoon of smoked paprika
- 3 cloves of crushed garlic
- 34g/2 tablespoons of mild curry powder

DIRECTIONS

1. Set your slow cooking appliance to the low setting.
2. Bring the oil to heat in a large frying pan before putting the onions in and allowing them to cook till transparent and soft.
3. Now throw in the parsnips and carrots, cooking them for 10 minutes till just golden.
4. At this point, add in the spices then let everything cook for 5 more minutes till they get fragrant.
5. If necessary add some water, mix through and toss everything into the slow cooker.
6. Throw in the bay leaves and lentils then adjust the seasoning accordingly.
7. Let everything cook for 5 hours until the broth is nice and thick and the veggies are tender.
8. Have a final taste of the seasoning and adjust if necessary before adding in the lemon juice.
9. Serve and enjoy with bread or rice.

Slow Cooker Vegetable Curry

Time: 6 hours 10 minutes | Servings 2
Kcal 391, Carbs 30g/1.05oz, Fats 22g/0.77oz, Proteins 11g/0.39oz, Fiber 14g/0.49oz

INGREDIENTS

- Whole meal flatbread for servings
- 500ml/2 cups can light coconut milk
- 1lime juice
- 51g/3 tablespoons of mild curry paste
- 160g/5.6oz frozen peas (defrosted)
- 8g/2 teaspoons of vegetable bouillon powder
- 15g/0.5oz of chopped coriander
- 1 red chili, sliced and deseeded
- 1 small aubergine sliced and chopped
- 17g/1 tablespoon of finely chopped ginger
- 1 red pepper, sliced and deseeded
- 3 sliced cloves of garlic
- 200g/7oz peeled and chopped butternut squash

1. Throw in the slow cooker the butternut squash, curry paste, coconut milk, garlic, bouillon powder, ginger, aubergine, and pepper then stir well then chill overnight.
2. Let everything cook for 6 hours till the vegetables are soft before stirring in the coriander the defrosted peas.
3. Add in the lemon juice to taste then serve with the flatbread.

Vegan Recipes

Slow Cooker Breakfast Beans

Time: 5 hours 30 minutes | Servings 4
Kcal 149, Carbs 21g/0.74oz, Fats 3g/0.1oz, Proteins 6g/0.21oz, Fiber 5g/0.17oz

INGREDIENTS

- A small bunch of chopped coriander
- 15ml/1 tablespoon of olive oil
- 250ml/1 cup of passata
- 1 thinly sliced onion
- 400g/14oz of drained and rinsed pinto beans
- 2 chopped garlic cloves
- 17ml/1 tablespoons of soft brown sugar
- 15ml/1 tablespoon of white or red vinegar

DIRECTIONS

1. Bring the oil to heat up in a large skillet before putting in the onions. Go on and fry the onions until they start turning brown.
2. Throw in the garlic and fry for another minute till they are nice and fragrant.
3. Now add the sugar and vinegar and allow everything to bubble up for a minute or 2.
4. Throw in the beans and passata stir well before seasoning with some pepper.
5. Transfer everything into the slow cooker.
6. Allow cooking for 5 hours in the low setting checking on the consistency of the sauce 20 minutes to time.
7. If the sauce is too thin for your liking, turn your slow cooker to the high setting and allow it to cook some more.
8. Finalize by throwing in the coriander and stir through before serving.
9. Enjoy with some brown bread on the side.

Slow Cooker Sweet Potato and Coconut Curry

Time: 6 hours 50 minutes | Servings 6
Kcal 434, Carbs 47g/1.65oz, Fats 22g/0.77oz, Proteins 6g/0.2oz, Fiber 10g/0.3oz

INGREDIENTS

- 34g/2 tablespoons of peanut butter
- 60ml/4 tablespoons of olive oil
- 500ml/2 cups of coconut milk
- 2 large sliced onions
- 300g/10.6oz passata
- 3 cloves of crushed garlic
- Cooked couscous
- 1kg/35oz of peeled and chopped sweet potatoes
- Thumb sized piece of chopped root ginger
- 250g/8oz of red cabbage
- 4g/1 teaspoon of paprika
- 2 sliced and deseeded red pepper
- 2g/½ a teaspoon of cayenne
- 2 sliced and deseeded red chili
- Small bunch of chopped coriander

1. Bring 15ml/1 tablespoon of oil to heat in a large skillet before putting in the sliced onions.

2. Allow cooking for 5 minutes or until the onions are slightly cooked before adding in the garlic and grate the root ginger right into the skillet.

3. Throw in the cayenne and paprika then cook for 2 more minutes before tossing everything into the slow cooker.

4. Add another 15ml/1 tablespoon of oil to the pan and add in the chili, cabbages, and red pepper.

5. Allow cooking for 5 minutes tossing frequently before tipping to the slow cooker.

6. Using the remainder of the oil, fry the sweet potato chunks on the skillet. Judging from the capacity of your pan, you may have to do so in more than one batch.

7. For roughly 5 minutes, cook the potatoes till they just begin to get color along the edges then transfer them to the slow cooker.

8. Empty the coconut milk and passata into the slow cooker and stir to mix everything up nicely.

9. Cook for 6 to 8 hours depending on the setting you choose on your slow cooker and cook till the sweet potatoes get tender.

10. Finally, add some peanut butter into the curry and stir. The heat should melt the peanut quickly.

11. Sprinkle the coriander atop and serve with some couscous.

Slow Cooker Pasta e Fagioli

Time: 6-8 hours 10 minutes | Servings 6
Kcal 225, Carbs 29g/1.02oz, Fats 6g/0.21oz, Proteins 10g.0.4oz, Fiber 9g/0.32oz

INGREDIENTS

- 30g/1.0goz parmesan vegan parmesan
- 200g/7oz of cannellini beans soaked for 6 hours
- 200g/7oz of cavolo nero with the leaves torn and stalks finely chopped
- 2 coarsely cut onions
- 150g/5oz of ditaloni rigati
- 3 chopped celery stalks
- 4 bay leaves
- 45ml/3 tablespoons of extra virgin olive oil
- 6 rosemary sprigs
- 4 crushed garlic cloves
- 34g/2 tablespoons of brown rice miso
- 1L/4 cups of vegetable stock
- 400g/14oz of plum tomatoes

DIRECTIONS

1. Drain the cannellini beans before boiling in salted water for 10 minutes.
2. Drain the salt water and rinse before putting in the slow cooker with the celery, onions, and carrots.
3. Add in the stock, olive oil sparing some for serving, garlic, tomatoes, miso, and some water then stir.
4. Using kitchen strings, tie the herbs together, and put them in.
5. Adjust the seasoning then allow cooking for 6 to 8 hours on the low setting till the veggies are nice and tender and the beans are cooked.
6. Remove the herbs before adding them to the pasta.
7. Now turn the slow cooker to the high setting and cook for an additional 30 minutes.
8. Toss in the cavalo nero leaves and stocks and finally allow cooking for 40 minutes still on the high setting.
9. To serve, grate the vegan parmesan atop before drizzling with some olive oil to your liking.

Vegan Chilli

Time: 6 hours 15 minutes | Servings 4
Kcal 365, Carbs 48g/1.7oz, Fats 10g/0.3oz, Proteins 12g/0.42oz, Fiber 17g/0.6oz

INGREDIENTS

- Lime wedges
- Chopped bunch of coriander
- Rice
- Guacamole
- 45ml/3 tablespoons of olive oil
- 400g/14oz canned kidney beans
- 2 sweet potatoes peeled and coarsely chopped
- 400g/14oz drained black beans
- 8g/2 teaspoons of smoked paprika
- 800g/28oz can of chopped tomatoes
- 8g/2 teaspoons of smoked cumin
- 1 red pepper sliced into chunks
- 1 chopped onion
- 15ml/1 tablespoon of tomato puree
- 2 chopped carrots
- 4g/1 teaspoon of dried oregano
- 2 chopped celery sticks
- 4g/1 teaspoon of chili powder
- 2 crushed garlic cloves

DIRECTIONS

1. Bring the oil to heat in a medium to a large frying pan over medium temperature.
2. Throw in the onions, celery, and carrots then allow them to cook for 10 minutes till they get nice and soft.
3. Now put in the crushed garlic and the sweet potato chunks then cook for 3 more minutes till they get nice and fragrant.
4. Put in the dry spices, tomato puree, and dried oregano then let everything cook for a minute or 2 before you transfer to the slow cooker.
5. Throw in the chopped tomatoes and bell pepper before stirring everything up in the slow cooker.
6. Now turn your slow cooker to the low setting, cover, and allow the mixture to cook for 5 hours.
7. Once the 5 hours elapsed, add in the beans and allow cooking for an additional 30 minutes to 1 hour.
8. Taste and adjust the seasoning accordingly before serving with the lime wedges, rice, and guacamole.
9. Sprinkle the chopped coriander atop and enjoy it!

Slow Cooker Masala Lentils

Time: 6 hours 10 minutes | Servings 8
Kcal 378, Carbs 57g/2.01oz, Fats 6g/0.21oz, Proteins 20g/0.7oz, Fiber 10g/0.3oz

INGREDIENTS

- Rice quinoa for serving
- 1 chopped yellow onion
- A pinch of black pepper
- 3 minced garlic cloves
- 6g/1½ teaspoons of garam masala
- 4g/1 teaspoon of ground ginger powder
- 4g/1 teaspoon of salt
- 300g/2¼ cups of green or brown lentils
- 5ml/1 teaspoon of maple syrup
- 1L/4 cups of vegetable broth
- 8g/2 teaspoons of tamarind paste
- 420g/15oz can of diced tomatoes with its juices
- 60ml/¼ cup of tomato paste
- 250ml/1 cup of light coconut milk

DIRECTIONS

1. Add every ingredient but the coconut milk in the slow cooker.

2. Switch it to the low setting and cook for 6 hours or on the high settings and cook for 3 to 4 hours. Be sure to have a look if the lentils require more water during the last 1 or two hours and add water or broth accordingly. Remember that you will still add coconut milk which could still cook the lentils.

3. After 6 hours or when the lentils are done, pour in the coconut milk and allow it to simmer for a short while before switching off the slow cooker.

4. Serve the lentils atop the quinoa rice and garnish with some fresh herbs.

Printed in Great Britain
by Amazon